Mighty

Written by Patricia Roberts

Contents

PEARSON

The Might of Machines

People build tunnels, bridges, roads and tall buildings in many places. Sometimes they build these with the might of machines.

Machines help people dig tunnels deep under the sea or through mountains. They can lift things that are heavier than a house. They can help people with jobs such as fighting fires or logging trees. Many of the mighty machines that people use have special jobs to do.

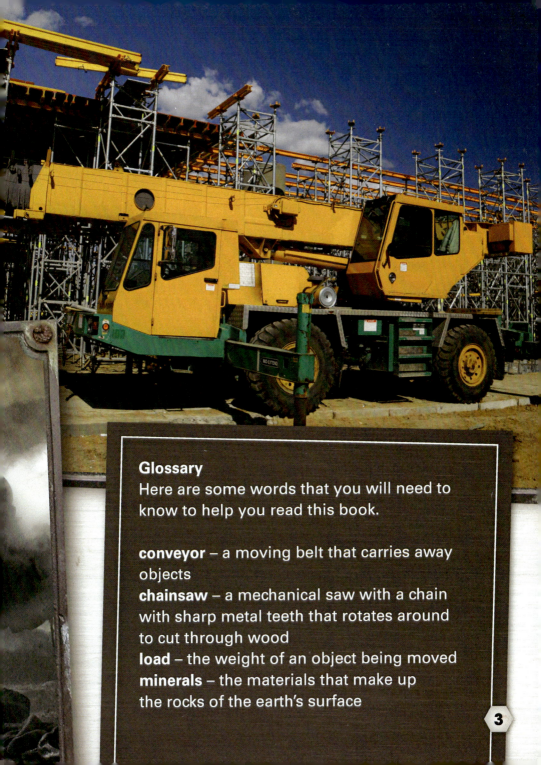

Glossary
Here are some words that you will need to know to help you read this book.

conveyor – a moving belt that carries away objects
chainsaw – a mechanical saw with a chain with sharp metal teeth that rotates around to cut through wood
load – the weight of an object being moved
minerals – the materials that make up the rocks of the earth's surface

Mighty Tunneller

When people wanted to build a tunnel, they would often blow up a mountainside with gunpowder! Today, there is a mighty machine called a tunnel-boring machine.

This mighty machine is like a giant drill. It digs into hard rock with a cutter. The cutter turns slowly and slices into the rock.

Rock

Cutter

Engine

Mighty Excavator

Some machines dig into the ground to reach minerals.
These machines are called bucket-wheel excavators.
A bucket-wheel excavator may have 24 buckets
around it. The buckets scoop up dirt and rocks.
Then a conveyor carries the dirt and rocks away
from the cutting site.

Conveyor

Tracks

Bucket

The buckets are often as big as a person. Some are even as big as a car!

Mighty Trencher

This machine is called a chain trencher.
It digs thin, deep trenches through rocks and dirt
so that pipes can be buried under the ground.

A trencher looks like a giant chainsaw. The cutting
teeth (or blades) are on a chain that moves around
wheels. The wheels are on a long arm that goes into
the ground. The chain trencher moves slowly forward
as it cuts through the ground.

Blades

Chain

The dirt and rocks shoot out one side of the chain trencher onto the ground above.

Arm

Chain

Felling head

Cabin

Chainsaw

Mighty Logger

Some mighty machines work in forests. A machine that cuts down trees does many jobs. It uses a felling head on the end of a long pole to hold a tree trunk. Then a large chainsaw cuts through the trunk. Blades take off the trunk's branches.

Some tree-cutting machines can cut and strip a tree every 15 seconds.

Blades

Tracks

 Mighty Hauler

Around the world, huge trucks work at mines. These mighty haul trucks can have six to eight huge tyres. They have two tough tyres at the front and four at the back. The tyres are made to ride over sharp, rough rocks and deep holes in the ground. The haulers carry big, heavy loads to and from the mines.

Cabin

Tyre

Ladder

Haul trucks are so large that the driver has to use a ladder to climb up into the cabin.

13

Mighty Transporter

The mighty crawler-transporter machine can be found at a space centre. It takes the space shuttles to the launch pad. The trip can take about six hours. The transporter crawls at about 1.5 kilometres per hour.

These giants are the largest machines that move on tracks. There are eight tracks, two huge tracks at each corner.

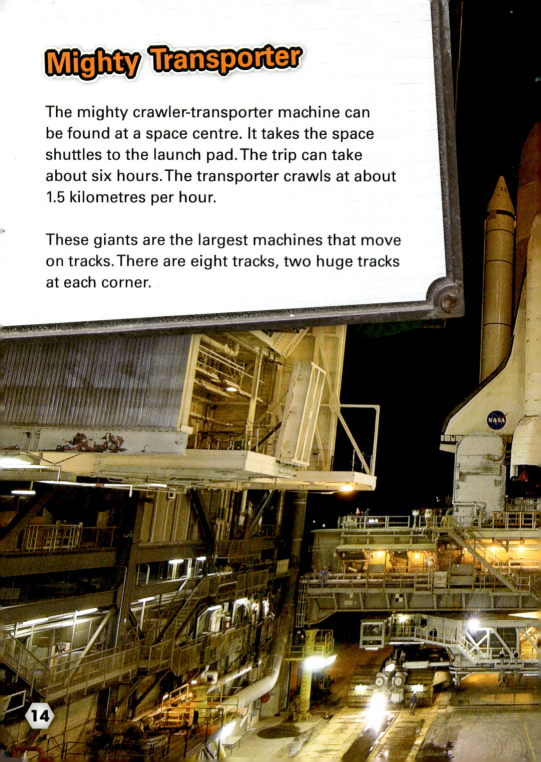

Discovery

Cabin

Tracks

It takes about thirty people to operate a crawler-transporter.

Summary Chart

Mighty Machine	What It Does
Bucket-wheel excavator	Digs into ground and scoops away dirt and rocks
Chain trencher	Digs trenches for pipes
Crawler-transporter	Used to transport space shuttles to a launch pad
Haul truck	Carries heavy loads in mines
Logger	Harvests trees
Tunnel-boring machine	Drills tunnels

Index

Reports

Mighty Machines is a Report.
A report has a topic:

Mighty Machines

A report has headings:

The Might of Machines

Mighty Tunneller

Mighty Excavator

Mighty Trencher

Mighty Logger

Mighty Hauler

Mighty Transporter

Some information is put under headings.

Mighty Transporter

It travels very slowly.
It has eight tracks.
It carries a space shuttle.

Information can be shown in other ways.
This report has . . .

Labels   Captions   Photographs   Summary Chart

Mighty Crawler-Transporter

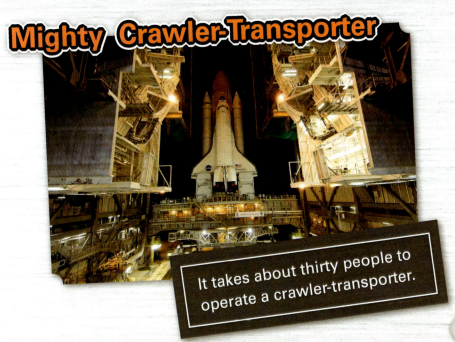

It takes about thirty people to operate a crawler-transporter.

▬▬▬ Guide Notes

Title: Mighty Machines

Stage: Fluency

Text Form: Informational Report

Approach: Guided Reading

Processes: Thinking Critically, Exploring Language, Processing Information

Written and Visual Focus: Contents Page, Labels, Captions, Glossary, Index, Summary Chart

THINKING CRITICALLY

(sample questions)

- What do you know about mighty machines?
- What might you expect to see in this book?
- What form of writing do you think will be used by the author?
- Look at the contents page and index. Encourage the students to think about the information and make predictions about the text content.
- Why do you think people use mighty machines?
- Why do you think the cutter on a tunnel-boring machine turns slowly?
- Why do you think the bucket-wheel excavator has a lot of buckets?
- What might the worker on a chain trencher have to look out for when digging a trench?
- Do you think tree logging could be dangerous with a tree cutter? What might happen?
- Why do you think the mighty crawler-transporter moves so slowly?
- What do you know about mighty machines that you didn't know before?
- What things in the book helped you understand the information?
- What questions do you have after reading the text?

EXPLORING LANGUAGE

Terminology

Photograph credits, contents page, index, glossary, imprint information, ISBN number

Vocabulary

Clarify: drill, excavator, site, trencher, strip, mines, transport, launch pad
Verbs: scoop, strip
Focus the students' attention on **adjectives, homonyms, antonyms** and **synonyms** if appropriate.